The Force Your Face Carries

A poetic novel by Angie Trudell Vasquez,
Poems from December 1994 to January 2001

For Barb! One of my kitties!
414-366-9003
♡ Angie

This book was designed by the author.
Cover photo by Aimee Pick

Art Night Books
2nd edition 2009
ISBN 978-0-979-4004-2-1

Some of these poems appeared previously as follows:

5th Annual Des Moines National Poetry Festival Chapbook: I Could Never, One Brown Face (formerly Color Contrast), Why I'm Dying

City View: I Could Never

Cuerpo: Lessons

Drake University Update Winter 1996: I Could Never

Iowa Humanities Board: One Brown Face

Jet City Maven: Facial

Our House: Human Maze

Periphery: Human Maze, One Brown Face, Poem for Men Who Think Their Wives Are Their Maids

Purgatorius.org: Alienation

Real Change: A Dream Within A Dream, Lessons, Living in the Jungle, Obituary for Tent City, Though This May Age Me a Hundred Million Years, Twiggyesque, Vanity, View at Jose Rizal Park and White Washer Plant Town

Stand Alone: Cursed, Dark Man, Dear John

The Times Delphic: One Brown Face

For Mary Avila Oliver and Juana Tovar Vasquez, my abuelitas.....

Contents

I. The Early Years, December 1994 to 1996

II. Love, 1997

III. Seattle, 1998-1999

IV. New Beginnings, 2000 to January 2001

Introduction by the Author/Acknowledgment

I finished the first version of this book in spring 2000. This is my first book. I make no apologies for the young girl, woman and women who appear among these pages. I cover nothing up but try to write as honestly as possible. It has changed many times since I first wrote it including the addition of the actual dates the poems were first written which tells the story better than I could by mere assemblage. I hope it touches you.

I want to thank the people who read my manuscript in its fledgling state and gave me feedback: Tricia (Vasquez) Young, Mindy (Anderson) Trudell, Melissa Rae Campbell, Esodie Geiger, Anissa (Baker) McNeece and Christine (Turner) Wilson, my father-in-law and poet Dennis Trudell and my husband, the cartoonist and humorist Devin Trudell. I want to thank the Iowa Public School System; my parents, Greg and Cherry Vasquez for nurturing my love of reading early on; my youngest sister, Sorral Vasquez, who attended many literary readings as a child; Jody Swilky, Drake University Professor, friend and mentor; Thomas Swiss, a Professor for Drake University who nominated me for Poetry's Ruth Lilly Poetry Fellowship; Rick Christman, a DMACC, (Des Moines Area Community College), professor who encouraged me to write; and last my deceased paternal grandmother, Juana Tovar Vasquez, who bought a seven year old girl a faux red leather diary for five dollars at a drugstore in downtown Newton, Iowa during summer vacation and started me on this writing journey.

Angela Christine Trudell Vasquez
February 27, 2005

I stand behind what I wrote previously.

Angela Christine Trudell Vasquez
November 21, 2008 2nd edition

Chapter I

The Early Years

December 1994-1996

One Brown Face

I am one brown face
in a sea of white.
I'm an American
in all the wrong spaces,
in the Midwest
of all places.
I eat yellow corn
and bale gold hay.
Detasseling,
like a migrant worker,
Gringo lover, that I am.
"You're so tan,"
my friends say
"Why can't I be that way?"

I make tortillas and beans
the old fashioned way,
with bacon lard and white flour.
I love such fattening body decay.
Fat runs through my veins
making me a frito bandito,
browning me inside and out.
My red chilis are drying
and my new blender waits
for the salsa-beat swirl
while my molcahuete and stone wait.

I am one brown face
striding forth
on two brown skinny legs.
(Do I go boldly
where no dark face
has gone before?)
I dance and dream
in my own hazy way
and play with the boys.

I wear my high heel
no nonsense
black patent leather shoes
and my stiff iron white shirt
while I tap my red nails
against the glass ceiling,
and wait for the great "Voleo"
to fall from the sky

to be replaced
by a colored guy
who'll create
the "Brown Boy System" someday
and have his own way
or so he say.

December 19, 1994

I Could Never

I could never
eat bloody caviar
or wear prancing horses
on my breasts
like my American comrades
who buy Jeep Cherokees,
life insurance
and watch
primetime TV
with its soaps and
minute by minute
live news casts
flashing naked bodies
lying upside down
with their feet
in gutters
and their heads
(off with their heads)
chopped off.

I could never
join the boy's club
rally for the football team,
and go "Rah Rah Rah"
vibrating my pompoms
and shaking my breasts
like my dear
American comrades.

I could never
give in to
lifeless living
sustained
by watching
trumped up characters
live (long I)
no live,
through glass screens,
prime time print,
and fuzzy reflections
distant from
Absolute Reality.
I could never.

February 7, 1995

Why I'm Dying

I'm crying because I'm dying
for a drink from
a tall frosted glass
filled with praise
brimming with hope as it splashes
down my throat.

I'm crying because I'm dying
for a top 40 hit song
playing on the radio waves
making me feel
like I want to dance
with a dark man from my past,
slowly.

I'm crying because I'm dying
for a long steamy glance
from the dark man of my past
hot enough to peel my clothes
off my smoking body
like a banana
and make me come.

I'm crying because I'm dying
for a hot summer day
to roll in the sand and
bake my body gold
so I can sell it
to the highest bidder
and become wealthy and old.

I'm crying because I'm dying
to laugh so hard
my sides split out
and I lose my breath
as my intestines
collapse in a heap
at my feet
and we all fall down,
entangled.

I'm crying because I'm dying
to have a job
where my talents
are used not wasted
where my brain doesn't emit

a slow smoke-like vapor
which pours creativity
through my ears and nose
until it's all gone.

I'm crying because I'm dying
for someone
to make me feel
like a human again
after I've reclaimed my humanity
while almost dying from
the brink of pain
and the joy of life beginning.

I'm crying because I'm dying
for pure undiluted
oil-like happiness
sold in tiny crystal
clear cut bottles
at Macy's perfume counter
ready and available
anytime 24 hours a day
for the ones you love.

March 21, 1995

Human Maze

Don't hate me because I'm brown,
my people worshipped the sun for years,
sacrificing their village virgins,
eating their dead, calculating sums
beyond mathematicians greatest dreams,
until their brain power grew beyond them,
dividing men from women until
it became the world's standard practice,
multiplying faster and faster,
creating more brown and white people
by way of electronic brain waves,
(Certainly not foreplay, friar man).

Until the world grew too small for the
human race population and a
new white people were born to weed the
garden and bury the dead, and who
did such a good job, the ground became
full of rotting corpses and mixed blood,
which mixed with the soil infecting
the oils of men and women through fruits,
green vegetables and flowers with sweet
smelling body heat and hot human
juices, which flowed through their nostrils, and
slid down their throats to land in a pool,
a pit, where benevolent white souls
purge bodies with a kiss and trickle
of purity steam, first invading,
then penetrating, and lifting their
lily white bodies up from earth just
like our language and food infiltrates English.

March 28, 1995

Climaxes

There are times
when we meet
somewhere
between the sheets
where our bodies
collide
and
our minds divide
then retreat
to the back
of our brains
where they hover
like aliens,
until we're too tired
and we tumble
bodies reaching,
stretching limb
over arched body,
fucking
like two teens
after prom
in the back of a Chevy
out of our minds,
into our bodies,
through our souls
where we meet
in between the sheets
just sex
yes,
it's a spiritual thing.

Spring 1995

Out

I'm flattered that it mattered,
for you to tell me
you were in love.
My heterosexual dreams
fried and died inside,
but I survived
and found
I loved you more
for your liberal logic
and human strain,
than for your
masculine brain.
We were equal
you and I,
no sexual tension
hovered between us,
feminism our freedom
it too liberated you
my friend
and we talked
on equal footing,
we were rose blooms
opening up to
receive the rain
our minds talking,
our mouths walking,
our tongues clicking
against the roof
of our mouths
as we made up
for lost time
two mates,
male and female,
friends not lovers,
we shared dreams
and discovered
we were on
the same team
long confined
by our work mind,
stuffed in an
artificial atmosphere,
where we hid
our true feelings,
we drank a pitcher of beer,
and made up

for twelve months
of silence
with loose lips
and open hearts,
until we were kicked out
by the bartender.
I'm flattered that it mattered,
for you to tell me
you were gay.

Spring 1995

Cursed

Beauty is power
and power is knowledge
of the force your face carries
(which eludes you)
among strangers,
spectators and
seeing-eye violators
(who don't even know you
but judge you the same)
I watch them bow
beneath your beauty,
the external force
you press upon them,
corrupting their flesh
with your physical warmth
and god-given fire,
which spreads shedding
pink charisma buds
everywhere you go
like a blanket of snow
covering the crowd
as you float past.

People want to know you
touch your body
and soil their hands
on your unblemished torso,
to become privy
to what's beneath
your clothes as if they
could steal your glow
for themselves
while you're not looking
borrowing against
the grain of your person,
the tilt of your nose
and widespread
commercial appeal.
But they wouldn't
if they only knew
the trouble
your beauty brings you
and the man you're
sworn to love until
death do you part—

or until he kills you—
because someone wants you to
display what's behind
your made up veneer,
angelic makeup exterior
and paper-thin smile,
hallowed by some,
coveted by more than one,
hollowed by years
of female competition
and men's knowing exhibition
in the back of their cars
honking on their pickup horns
while their parents are sleeping.

Poor child,
poor girl
you had a nice body too.
But you were a slut
before you knew it,
even though no one proved it,
and your peers
preferred the worst—
because everyone just knew
young
bodacious girls
were just bimbos,
put on this televised earth,
to visually please,
tease, then freeze,
"Oh no, please stop"
and jerk off their dates
over the phone.

Because big brains
don't mix with big tits,
round hips
and lush red lips
which pucker
and color
all on their own;
without lipstick
impressions or
silicon injections
for the popular
pouty look,
and because

you had a fucking brain,
because you named the source
of all your pain,
you began to stutter
and shudder every time
you looked into a mirror
until you fell into your grave
a Snow White mannequin.

May 1995

Poem for Men Who Think Their Wives are Their Maids

Don't fucking yell at me,
you yellow-backed
mother-fucker,
who
can't get off his
ass
to get a beer
from the refrigerator
only three feet away.

Because I'm tooting,
I'm scooting,
I'm moving off your land,
your domain,
your castle,
where you're king.

I'd rather be
a big butt bitch
than your
little candy ass.

I've burned your
last dinner,
and hidden
all of your hooch,
you couldn't get a rise
out of me
if you cut
off all of my hair,
because I'm leaving
you for a higher plain
where big strong men
don't parade and
aren't afraid
of the women
that I am.

August 26, 1995

Dark Man

I see you mirrored
in your black suited brothers,
walking erect down
high-curving tax-paid city
streets grazing the
bottom of the glass ceiling
pushing back with
the strength your mother did when
she enrolled you in
primary school, walking down
the cold hallways
not speaking any English,
yet, neither do you,
but she fought the white people
weak as she was.

She knew America would
teach you as if
you were their own child, molding
your shape to be
a brown man with a white mask
who could make it
in the service, in college
and on Wallstreet's floor,
where you'd fight for the privilege
to make money,
and send your daughters to school
where they'd succeed,
and surpass your need to show
how you could grow
close to the scent of money.

January 1996

Explanation

I write in code
mask my feelings
from all eyes to see
among words, verbs
and parentheses.
Souls part and expand
to a rhythm not human,
beings aren't given
to understand
its literal meaning
stuck in this primordial
recess called Earth,
and I spring dead words
from my mind
on to the remainder
of a tree and pray
for forgiveness
of all sins
I commit
in thought and deed.

January 10, 1996

Watching, Wanting

I watch your lips
as they move
sideways
across your face
when you talk
to me
about things
other than love:
profit margins,
taxes, raises,
proper protocol,
progress reports.

Firm, moist,
horizontal for life,
I wish to touch that
half -flesh- skin
awake, infuse it
with my tongue.
I sit, stare, watch
you dare me
with your speech,
lips, mouth
moving south
tempting me
to kiss it quiet
make you silent.

February 27, 1996

Escapism

I rise above your anger,
float on a smoke cloud
I call heaven and inhale
until the cows come home,
glad to be alive
and in the free world,
where pot can be bought
for $20 bucks a shot
from the man
at the coffee stand
on the corner of 12th & Grand
so I can free float,

high,

above your steam.

March 18, 1996

Lessons

She walks through yellow fields, migrant worker,
bronze goddess, reaper of corn, not worthy
of our scorn, as we mourn her callused hands
and turn away afraid it might be catching.

She weaves a web protecting her dead children
from memory loss, preserving the story
of their demise in rich red cloth,
woven by hand, washed with tears, soaked
in blood, then sold to western tourists who
can't understand how a son or daughter disappears.

She works at a factory sweating
for fifty cents an hour, pressing the clothes
rich women will buy to hang in their closets
and not on their slim well fed tan bodies
as they stroll on easy street never breaking a nail.

She buys cafe mochas for $2.50
from the man in the stand
by the corner before driving
through rush hour to work downtown
not savoring the aroma of brown backs
burning in the sun bending to pick
beans one-by-one selecting only
the choicest ones to sell on the
American slave market.

Spring 1996

Dear John

I don't want to alarm you,
but my skin is falling off
in secret private patches
you once kissed with your tongue.

(No! Don't go see a doctor yet.
Let me explain.)

You see, when the moon was full
I danced to the tune of the insane
in my backyard, naked and unashamed,
when my tongue suddenly tripped on your name.

My brain refrained
from the steamiest details of our passion,
now out of fashion
and I danced and I danced,
until I shed you piece by piece
turn by turn, matter by matter,
like a bad hang nail.

Unburdening myself,
I was, I was, to the moon, the cool green grass and
my neighbors, Mr. and Mrs. Sane,
(who watched me open mouthed through their kitchen
window pane).

I flew into a kinetic frenzy,
twirling to the tune of the insane,
naked and unashamed,
free of your atoms
as they blew off my body,
with the beat of my heart,
and the buzz of my brain,
as I danced and pranced,
until I knew when the music
stopped on a beat,
I didn't want you.
You can't dance.

August 20, 1996

Poison

I fear
the venom
you spit
that spills
from your mouth
as you hurl
words at me
like bricks
from a bridge
you create
far away
from me,
from reality.

Come back
and share
my dream
where we lay
in bed
in the middle
of the day
and make love
as only free
married people do:
without guilt,
without pain,
without plastic.

September 15, 1996

Gender Games

The personal is political
and I thought you might
need reminding:
I don't iron your clothes
or cook your dinner
or put your socks
away in neat little bundles,
so you can dress more easy,
I am your wife, and
I have a life and that's the way
it must be, for I am
no Charlotte Perkins Gilman wannabe
crawling across yellow wallpaper,
because I'm not free to think
or write or have autonomy.
I can mope, vote, have sex or smoke.
I can even own, sell or buy
my own property.
I am free of old
male patriarchal fantasies.
Women are more than their
biological tendencies,
the pleasing planes of their face,
the stem of their tree.
We are human,
we are flesh,
we are free,
though not intellectually favored
throughout history,
but not now you see,
and that's why your free time
is not important to me.

1996

Waiting

I sit at home,
read and write alone,
while you are somewhere else
tearing up our home,
but no that's me
and my free thinking ways.

I wait for the sound
of the sliding glass door opening.
What will I do
when I don't have you,
and you sit and adorn
someone else's room
with your long pale face?

1996

Chapter II

Love

1997

Babysitting

When my Morgalou was two
she sat on her Titi's lap and wreaked havoc
with her paper, baby scissors and blue ink pen,
"Whoopsie Daisy" she said.
She stapled bits of paper with glue,
colored with pink and yellow markers
then declared in her outside voice,
"I must write! I must write!"
and proceeded to draw a picture
Picasso like, when I read this to her just now
out loud, she said "Cool."

January 1997

On Why I Could Never Marry You

After another family wedding
my mother calls to tell me
you asked about me,
if I was still married and
I remember the first night we met
at a family wedding,
you were with my cousins
a white boy who liked to play "mercy"
with the girls just to hold hands,
you were my friend,
and it was you who held
my heart in your hand
after the man I loved
crushed it to pieces,
yet you never took advantage.
I loved you then for being my friend
and remember the time you swore
your love eternally in ink pen,
gave me a note in high school
between classes, and how I said,
"But Meredith you're my friend"
and how that must have hurt.
I remember scraping our knees
when we climbed trees
in Iowa City like children
even though we were old enough to drink
our way through college.
Now 12 years later,
I still marvel at your desire
wonder how I sparked your fire
if you'll let me in.

March 17, 1997

Morgan

When you were born red and messy
and I watched the hygienic white nurses
wash your paper thin newborn skin,
stab you with their life preserving needles,
I realized how strange this must have been
for you to leave your mother's warm liquid body
and enter our cold clean antiseptic world
with alcohol, drugs and dirty movies
24 hours a day, every day
available on all street corners
where already you were worth
$3000 dollars of medical bills, even though
you couldn't yet see with your newborn baby eyes
and I, as your aunt, saw how pure you were, mija,
and swore to help protect you from
the harsh realities of this earthbound existence,
as long as I live and breathe.

March 18, 1997

The Glance

Black eyes smolder as you look
upon my naked breasts
bra torn off for your gaze
met by mine as I stroke
my fingers on your bold member
and sigh this is not enough,
once is not enough.

I see you tremble with desire,
my hands long to touch
your Black-Irish-soul-being
until my fingers are bloody
from strumming your body
like a guitar until I know
the tune so well,
I could play it by heart
in my head and in my bed
while I dream of your eyes.

Good Friday, April 1997

Erasure

Life's erased just like that
words once spoken
are vows broken
dissolve into paper
at my feet.
I gladly tromp
upon them
smashing my feet
like the mash potato
shedding those thick skins
against the concrete
dusty dirty remains
of my unpopular marriage
now transparent.

June 10, 1997

I'm a Scarred Scared Woman

He drove by just now,
    "stalker-fear-feeder-man,"
a piece of paper declares
my peaceful existence,
but I don't see how,
    "stalker-fear-feeder-man."
Tomorrow, I will march
to the courts, lay my claim
for a place of my own
to read, write, think all alone,
full thoughts, complete sentences,
white space cushions all around me,
covering me with their verbal blessings,
    "No stalker-fear-feeder-man."
And I? I wait for the moment
I can't conjure up his face,
the desire I first felt in his arms,
when we were just beginning,
before he started thinning,
stopped grinning and
I blossomed on my own.

Summer 1997

Facial

Peeling back the layers
like an orange
I look for myself
beneath the veins
and pulpy surfaces.

Summer 1997

A Dream Within A Dream

At a summer swimming party
I pull myself out of blue water
and see my Grandma Alice
watching the orange sun set,
her fine white head is turned to the side,
her meaty thighs billow beside her.
I walk towards a round green glass table,
where my Grandma Mary and Juana sit
eating beans and tortillas,
drinking yellow lemonade.
I tell them about my idea:
to open a center to teach
immigrants standard English,
so they can get better jobs,
make a better life for their families,
fulfill the American dream,
and my blind Grandma Mary
looks at me straight in the eyes,
smiles broadly showing all her teeth, and says
"I think that's a wonderful idea."
And my Grandma Juana, who seems to have
lost her ability to speak English,
nods as if to say, yes,
you are the one who can link us,
and I don't know if it's because
Grandma Mary and Alice are alive,
and I'm in her dream, or if it's
because she believes in me.

Summer 1997

Journal Entry in the Day of an Iowa Woman

Today I woke up
walked to the Farmer's Market
downtown with my two sisters,
my mother and my niece
who's not yet three.
I bought red-ripe cherry tomatoes
that burst to the touch,
round orange hairless nectarines,
George's fresh baked Italian bread,
green snappy jalapenos, and
homemade Amish cinnamon bread,
but none could compare
with my niece's little skin.
She smells like only the very young can,
fresh, yet unsoiled
by our polluted earth
with it's stale air of
funky cars, cigars, cigarettes,
body odor, perfume and fear.

Summer 1997

Love Chat

I present myself to you
on a platter, all perfumed
powdered and ready
for skin to skin sin-pleasure.

Your pulse is warm to mine,
I feel the power of your pull,
your sex desire and I unfold
like a flower, lips and thighs part.

My tongue soul searches,
I melt close to your heart
until I'm liquefied inside,
and we become one thrust,
one rhythm, one pulse beat
as we dance and make love chat.

July 21, 1997

Remember

I seek in my mind
I search for the time
we were together
flesh to flesh:
my arms akimbo,
we stood on a bridge
I didn't want to trek
you started across
I followed until sure
then leapt on my own
across the rocks
like a dancer,
not taking your hand
I preferred to cross alone,
independent of any man,
yet I called out your name
"Devin."

I search my mind
for the time we were together
swimming in the green lake
happy to be alone, away from
the heat of the sun our friends
spectator-eyes, as we splashed
and laughed in the green foam,
and kissed and kissed until I was
embarrassed to be a shameful
wanton wise woman
making love to a man
I'd only known ten days,
ten great days.

I search my mind and seek
for the time we were together
when you kissed my breasts,
the curve of my stomach,
the insides of my thighs,
my tender lips.
I sighed with pleasure
knew we were together
when I too wanted to hold you
close in my mouth and did,
displaying my desire
for your maleness
your hard member,
I knew you wanted me

the way I want you
my heaven lover,
the man I dream about
who holds me secure,
leads me to shore safety
with his artist arms and hands,
hands I want to caress me,
lips I want to kiss me,
thighs I need close to me,
a heart I can admire.

July 27, 1997

Domestic Nightmare

I heard you asked if I was at the fair.
I dare say you wanted to see me there
I know because I heard the urge in you
when you said it hurt to see my shape
across the field after I accepted your call
late one night when I was feeling weak and lonely.
Your words still twist in my mind all gray and cloudy.
Where did I place my brain during those early years?
Perhaps we were a lesson for our friends to see
a quick recall for those long buried in the burbs,
where they slave for money most days
forget to pray for independence
working to pay the rent or mortgage,
living a minivan man woman existence:
golf, beer, mowing on the weekends
or a fate worse than death a lifetime
membership to the best country club;
but back to you ex-husband, former friend and foe,
where evil man sits and demands-demands-demands
to be let go, you see it's all my fault, even when it's not,
remnants of a bad marriage haunt my dreams
make me wake up to see what time it is.

August 18, 1997

For the Record

You made me sleep less in Seattle
when we broke the world's record
for the longest deepest kiss,
since black and white movies.

You made me laugh like a hyena in Madison
after we drove around green town
bobbing our heads like puppets on a string
to reggae's beat, boom box astride on top forgotten.

You made me learn to love your smell
when you came and loved me in Iowa,
confusing my life with joy and honesty,
a rare treat for a woman who was beat.

You made my heart beat too fast,
I can't keep up with the past
and let it roll over me
when our lips and hips crash.

Now you're my lover
my best friend among men,
a body I cling to in a storm
of emotions, a man I can trust.

September 1, 1997

Limbo

I didn't wash the sheets
when you left
but slept in them and
breathed our mingled
scents all night long.
In the morning,
I called in to work with the flu,
dreamed about you 'til noon,
when I awoke
the smell of your sweat
was on my left shoulder.
I chose not to bathe
so I could lean down my nose,
smell you closer.
I lay on my bed
remember how it felt
to wake up and smile at you
instead of myself all alone
living a sterile life
in between the times
I'm in your arms,
waiting for your call.

Fall 1997

Red Blooded Hate

I write in red
like the color
of the dream
deep in my head,
but no, it's my heart,
and I remember
his long southern drawl,
the summer I was twelve,
how his words came out like a river stone
all even and smooth, good proper English,
and they touched me via electronic brain waves,
white hats galloped across my mind
like in Margaret Mitchell's Gone With The Wind,
they come close, so close my throat constricts
as I hear this pretty white boy say,
"They should all go back to where they came from."
The reporter spouts off about his straight A's,
zoom in on this summer camp
that teaches kids how to fire guns,
prepare for the war against the races,
the invasion of the coloreds,
and I feel it bounce off me,
bury deep in my blood,
pumping blue anger
it courses through my veins,
and right or wrong I loathe his pasty face
wish he'd die and that scares me more
than any pointed hood riding in a herd of ignorance.

Fall 1997

Fallen Woman

Fallen woman fears no one
she fingers neighbor folk
as she floats by
high on her ability
to walk alone,
buy her own smoke
court love in her heart
caress it like a white dove
be serene
in the face of poverty.

Fallen woman falls no more
there's no safety net now,
she only has herself to blame
or pick herself back up,
and despite what the woman
next door tells her
there's no shame
in returning to your maiden name.

She's fallen from married grace
the suburban urban myth,
to rise once more
shaking off the floor
as the girl next door
flooded with red ripe
possibilities, pregnant
like the full moon:
filled with round hope.

October 16, 1997

While Smoking on my Porch

(for Melissa)

While smoking on my porch,
I watched a parade of pretty people pass by
jogging after seven, sweating, no perspiring
in their designer sweats and latex shoes,
and it was apparent to me no one had a clue about
what was what or true, and if they had any inkling
it was squashed by two at the homeless golf course
on a Friday afternoon under the blazing sun
after a beer or two, yes, the soulless wonders were
hard at networking, feeding the status quo,
making underhand deals to let the rich get richer,
and the poor more in debtor leaving a good base
to romp on, stomp on, feel good about, yes,
the pretty party people blew by before they dressed
and dined out for dinner.

October 16, 1997

2nd to Last Supper

When I left Iowa in December snow was falling
and I was bawling because I knew it would be too long
before I saw their round brown smiling faces sitting
around the dinner table eating our own version of Mexican food:
chicken mole, beans with fresh garlic and onion,
hand made still warm fresh flour tortillas;
this is what love is made of good conversation
about our brown and white uprising while the steam
off the food is rising to fill our tongues, our throats, our stomachs,
then out of the blue my little niece Morgalou coos,
"Titi, but where are you going?" and I said "Seattle."

Winter 1997

Though This May Age Me a Hundred Million Years

For you I'll take off my armor wear my naked face and feel pretty,
for you I'll cross the US in an '89 Mustang with all our possessions,
for you I'll face my fears when snow and ice plague the road,
though it may age me a hundred million years,
for you I'll leave home become a world class traveler
and make the world our playground,
for you I'll quit my job, relocate 2000 miles away,
for you I'll remember how to roar again with laughter
after hundreds of miles drunk off beer and deep tongue kisses,
with you I'll smoke until we're old and gray
passing the coffee can, rolling our own Js,
with you I'm free to remember who I am
who I was and who I want to be
with you I'm not afraid to face the truth,
and spread sunshine as we drive
state to state ever west ever loved
as we stop, gas up and go on and on.

December 7-15, 1997

Taking Inventory

I'm 30 and my life runs in front and behind me,
telling me this story, now that, whispering old secrets,
reluctant half truths and misnomers,
sometimes I'm married to a brat,
sometimes I'm drowning in tears,
sometimes I'm the smartest girl in the class,
then I flee fly free to Seattle
with a man I met just yesterday
where I fall in love until I'm dazed
by his taste, the touch, the smell of his skin
where we laugh so much I have to pee, and
swear to Jesus there never was a man so funny
in this magical green land where true love grows
tall like the pine trees into blissful domestic harmony,
where I blossom each day with a smile
blessed out because I'm free of misery
for my life stretches out in front of me
and I see green for miles and miles.

Winter 1997

Chapter III

Seattle

1998 - 1999

Checking Out

I travel around in my mind
and find I'm not so different than
I was then, there's just more of me
though I'm so thin my mother asks me
if I'm eating, do I need money, am I depressed,
and I smile happy with my skin and bones
and reply, "Yes, I'm doing fine all alone.
Rice and beans are my staples."
I don't tell her the faint smell
of bacon fat wrapped around
the brown bean's juice of life
is enough to make me cry
and forget about mariachi music,
I'm all tears then, and wet-black velvet eyes
and if someone touches me just right
I'll break down and soliloquize
about how I miss fields of yellow corn,
how they're thin green arms waved in the wind,
and how me and my soul sisters danced
by the light of the moon carried away
by Tito Puente's band, our bare feet and gin.

March 1998

Because I Recycle

When you tell me why you left
I don't listen to your words
but think back to a previous life
where I lived my best years
strapped to the back of some man
I made the mistake of marrying
it takes me a long time to realize
you are speaking the truth
I don't want to hear
what you have to say,
I pretend I'm upset
or you're criminally insane,
but it doesn't work in this place
and I have to find a new way
to communicate with men
I'm involved with since
I'm all alone in this space
I call heaven but it's far from home
and I have to recreate myself from dust
no parochial rib will get in the way
this time because I'm turning
into stone like a pillar of salt
no one can touch the spot
I call my brain but I may give
them a piece of this much used-heart.

Spring 1998

Soulmates

When you see into my eyes
and know I think
you are someone
I've never seen before,
and realize why I behave
real peculiar now and then,
don't tell me I'm not scared
to be in love with you,
until I can't sleep at night
without wondering when
paradise will end
and at what price,
and ask God why
do I believe all good things
must come to an end,
and recall telling someone else,
"I'd mourn you more than all the rest"
and meaning it,
but I feel it more about you
because you said,
"Should I be right"
and 'God' recreates us
into another image,
you would find me,
and then at that moment
we agreed to find each other
in the next lifetime,
it was then at that moment
when I knew it was you
I was meant to share my life with.

Spring 1998

Sugar

He done left my dog
outside in the rain
for twelve hours all day
from 9AM to 9PM
my dog was stuck in the rain
and I had a clear vision today
saw my Sugar girl
outside in the mud howling
while Seattle dripped
its tears on her white fur,
thin pink skin,
bunny rabbit ears,
like me she's a princess
but she can take a pounding,
we both overcame,
we escaped the violence
we shared through one man,
our old man, not the one
we have now,
he's a good man,
he just forgot I taught
ESL tonight at the church
thought I'd come home
on lunch and get her,
or didn't want to mess
with her just then
and walked to work
obsessed instead
with the thoughts
in his head so
she stayed outside,
cried probably barked,
whinnied for her mommy
to come home
and save her.

Spring 1998

Napoleona

My Morgaloo is only four
and yet she controls me
when I'm home,
telling me which dress to wear
which one looks better
and we negotiate from there.

"Titi, wear your button dress."

"How about the green one?"

"Okay, that looks good too."

Out the door hand in hand to the store
with faithful Wishbone we go
but that's a mistake because
I look like a stick woman
battling some swordsman
running down the street
dragging a tiny baby in tow
my minute commander,
who is only four,
who I must turn to and plead,
"Hija, no es puedo."

June 1998

Sweet Scent

I can smell the sweet scent of my own sweat
as I blow high with the breeze and swing,
I pump my legs like a child again my skinny kid's butt
holds me down, keeps me grounded
when adults threaten to pull me off.
My chain breaks as I tempt to kiss the sun,
my knees have a life of their own bending
as if my very existence depended on it,
and it does, for I'd rather be a nut flying high
over people's heads than on the ground dying
touching the earth, staining the water
with my unclean mind, my hands washing red
off the money so I can sleep off my power trip
and back stabbing toys.
I was an old soul at five spouting off
about the filth of my generation.
I knew greed was the root of all evil,
competition its close cousin.
I had my doubts about civilization as I found it
and convinced my sister Tricia to wear
flannel jammies zipped to the throat in the summer
to protect us from the babysitter's bloodsucking
husband while our parents went out for supper.

July 2, 1998

Mind Candy

Mind candy loses flavor
if you suck on it too long,
just like too chewed gum.
I find myself stuck
in a strawberry swirl shake,
and all I can do is go home and bake
and write poem after poem
until I find myself among the words
living in between the lines.

July 7, 1998

Never More

Love doesn't live here anymore
I kicked her out the door,
she made me weep,
she left me weak. I repeat.

Love doesn't live here anymore,
I'm all sore, my heart's broke,
and I can mope for days on end,
but I won't let her back in the door.

September 30, 1998

First Fight

After I talked to my friend
for an hour
and drank hot jasmine tea
the poison
scraped out of me,
filling my throat with its bile yellow taste,
I retched
until I couldn't catch my breath
it ran out in front of me like wildfire,
my cheeks and eyes
bled red,
the flavor of love gone sour,
dust, ashes
along the throat
that once lapped desire.

October 1, 1998

Support Manager Queens

Unstrap the chain,
unwrap the cellophane packages,
mask ourselves with
pretty war paint,
icicle smiles,
and push the broom
around for miles
as if we're working
long hard hours
playing men like desires
and rumpled gin rummy
with our short, short skirts,
naked white tooth smiles
and pretend, pretend
we're strong and tougher
than all the men
(our apelike predecessors)
and hollowed miles of years
where we sat demure
knit to and fro
from the kitchen
to the cellar
marking time,
bearing children,
spreading our legs
flat on our back
wearing nothing
but fake smiles.

October 16, 1998

Education

Advertising rots the brain,
tips the scale in the favor
of the small millions, and
weighs on the grand divide.
Little men play
on the blackboards
across the nations
dividing the jungles
of the crass masses:
you need yard tools
and play stations,
golf balls and white paper,
palm pilots and cubicles,
the lowest common
denominator
to appeal to
all ages and races.

Sell red hot sex,
moist wet lips and long moans,
people who drone on and on
about the benefits
you and your family
can retire on,
products that just can't miss
lies you can sleep on and
dreams to keep you going.
It benefits
the small few
who pretend it is you
they're most concerned for and why
can't you show up for work
when it's your daily labor
they depend on.

October 23, 1998

Twiggyesque

I cry when my sister
tells me why she's fat,
why our little sister's chubby,
why so many of us binge
and purge throughout the day
so we can be "Barbie-esque"
feel we are as beautiful
as frail doe eyed models,
who really need a sandwich,
who don't represent us,
the common woman anyway,
because she's a freak of nature
at six feet three and a 130,
because putting women on pedestals
sells more slinky lingerie, wedding gowns,
and little black strappy dresses
until time calls for plastic numbers:
breast lifts, tummy tucks, liposuctions,
permanent lipstick sheens
with sunscreen for day,
followed by night cream
religiously before bed
for lotion alcoholics who need their fix:
everyday, every minute of the hour,
glossy, retouched, airbrushed, stretched
zine models litter our capitalistic
scene on billboards, busses, and
grocery store check out counters
so a few make a fortune off
feeding women low self esteem
and we buy Lean Cuisine.

1998

Espresso Love

Steaming cups of breasts,
long lusty looks
over the lunch counter
frost white froth like lips,
warm smoke jazz on tune
down low, sweat on my brow,
now on your lips
as you kiss my forehead
uncurl your furrow
go for a refill.

1998

Alienation

Stranded, I feel stranded
and yet why should I?
I feel like I'm working all alone.
I don't mind that's nobody's home
I'm content with the decisions I've made
life is no big parade,
no yellow brick road Dorothy might take,
no, it's a misunderstood mass throttling in the throes
twitching this way and that to the country's national beat,
like puppets on a string waiting for the big-bam-boom-bing
earthquake
called a bomb let off by some boob,
some pigeon shaped small minded military man
or rather some other self-religious,
self-proclaimed closet prophet,
or perhaps
some short man syndrome steroids taking
testicles shrinking American made male,
who missed the feminist education of a kinder
more gentler nation who takes care of
the young, the old, the sick, the feeble,
feeds and clothes the poor,
and doesn't complain
about what a waste of money it is and all
when you can't play with it or threaten it
against somebody in a desert storm,
because your toys are bigger than their toys
and we have more economic resources
under our thumb
and can shit at will
anytime we please by a push of a button
from our leader in chief
or from one of our many multinational corporations,
those conglomerations
with their take no prisoners rhetoric
with men and women managers who pretend to be men,
who play let's see how much money we can spend then spit out
for our shareholders, the board of trustees,
without regard for earth or humans' destiny;
and they can do it because they own the store
the green bills stop in their store bought courts,
then justice is dumb, blind, deaf and stupid
unless you've got money, thank God,
there are some defense lawyers out there who care
and will fight to the death not to kill or scare
one more brother or native transsexual transient

for self-defense, hash quest or political imprisonment.
I'm typing too fast, my heart beats rash
we are flesh and blood world tourists passing time continuum
we are not dumb or dangerous if our basics are met.
But how can we be at peace with our lack of sustenance
our nagging social status, our crumbling free press
as we straddle the socio-economic stratosphere
gambling our lives against monopoly earned money
while unelected leaders do the back door draft dance
and talking heads say we don't have a chance?

April 2, 1999

Flashback, After a Bad Dream

Don't tell me it's over
when I can recall
how your glance would
fall on me, now and then,
when love showed through
your lips, your eyes, your penis
dripped with our juices.
You will remember me
your whole life and I you,
oh, evil one, first love of mine,
last man from which I'll recover.

June 10, 1999

Fairway

His sadness weighs on him
I can feel it seep out
the corner creases of his eyes,
his mouth, his mind
passersby ignore him
they don't know why
or stop
to consider his pain
on their way to tee off
Friday
planted on the green
clubs and drinks in hand,
"those people"
stroll the course
hit a white ball
scratch their own,
scream
"This is fun!"
while networking:
golf, the game avoidance,
takes space from the homeless,
parks from the people,
playgrounds where wannabe
rich rat bastards
prey on the wealth of a nation
the cheap lads and lasses,
give back a minimum wage
paycheck
let them carry the bag,
call it good business practice.

June 15, 1999

View at Jose Rizal Park

He walked to the park
took his chicken out,
began to wash before dinner,
the sun set over the Olympics
as he washed his hands
for five full minutes,
then he rinsed
his store bought chicken,
knees bent sitting
on his haunches
like old Vietnamese villagers,
he watched the sun's
last lavender light
slip into darkness
over the Sound,
his utensils rested
on his backpack,
his face forever brown
unnatural for his race,
his teeth white straight,
he was a man
with no shelter
for the night,
no matter,
he ate off a plastic plate,
counted himself lucky
with his fresh fruit and grains,
an art park scene floated nearby,
a short dark girl goes by
walking her tall white dog,
a chubby African boy
giggles on a swing,
and he feels lucky to be
counted again among the living,
safe, clean and warm,
human rays have replaced the sun
smiles all around,
he knows he'll rest soon
to rise once more
off the cold mother earth floor
to look for work downtown
by the Millionair's club,
once a name for swanky swells,
now a place for men
who need a day job,
to push the hunger away,

whet the whistle:
brown men, white men, black men,
sober drunks, men with a record,
illegal aliens, students of mine,
from Mexico, Guatemala, Honduras,
protected by an unwritten clause with the city,
allowing corporate welfare,
local independent contractors, restauranteurs
to benefit under the table.

June 23, 1999

Innocence Crushed

He's an innocent caught in the crush
in the rush for his life to begin,
to sit on the edge of his seat
bite his nails from fear of defeat,
wait for the tart treat beside him
to see him enraptured with
the first girl since mom,
he craves the excitement promised him
since he was in his early teens:
Mountain Dew commercial highs,
marshmallows oozing over the top
of his hot cocoa, the bad giggly woman
popping out of her brassiere on late night TV,
climbing an ice mountain may not be enough
for this tough, he'll have to feel the rush
you get from psychedelic drugs
mixed with marijuana, alcohol and lust,
later if he's lucky, he'll escape,
unpry death's beak
learn to use in moderation and fulfill
his full destiny as an angel
human being here on Earth.

July 1999

Vanity

She collects compliments
and horse whistles
like some women harbor
old love letters in their hearts,
so when she began to decay
leave her late forties,
and a man chanced to sashay
then say those three little words
lost in the throws of consummation
with that most wonderful verb thrown in
she flew into a rose colored frenzy
it clouded her vision and she threw
her money around with uncharacteristic
abandon, because her lost looks and charisma
cost her that much and she had been worth plenty
in her heyday perched at the end of the bar
when the market was good and her coins
still held their full value,
so when he went away and all
she had was his bills to pay
to remind her of his presence/presents
she collapsed in a heap at the feet
of her mirror mistress and cried,
"Why does this keep happening to me?"

August 14, 1999

Living in the Jungle

I was driving home
checking off my long list of failures:
working for a red-haired man
who didn't give me enough play,
sky high divorce debt to this day,
a car on it's last leg,
no money for rainy nights,
when I spied paused at a red light
an indigenous couple
drinking from a rarely scene public bubbler,
between 12th and Jackson,
dressed in long red flannel sleeves and blue jeans
on this rare Seattle summer day,
the man let the woman drink first
she drank long and lusty while he held the spout,
then she too held it for him to satisfy his thirst;
they filled a red pop can to the brim
with the cold clear clean life liquid we all are
before walking off hand in hand
plastic Safeway bags in the other
backpacks like crosses upon their backs.

August 18, 1999

To Thine Own Self Be True

Neither a borrower nor a lender be
keep thy money close to thee at all times,
recall Grandma Mary who though blind
knew where her purse was all the time.

Be careful whom you enfold your flesh to
the body is weak, so spirit must be strong
to guide thee in the quest of one's own
defined sense of skin to skin morality.

Forgive your self when you fall
it will be free and plenty
learn from disaster ashes
and work towards your moment goal.
this way you never have to say,
I could have but for lack of trying.

Recall the ant that stores his bread knowledge,
there's no free meal, there's a price to pay,
and to live well one must work in some shape
on the field, in the building or on the pavement.
all work's the same, unless it's your art.

Feed your mind, feed your soul, feed your body
all life must eat so eat wisely.
Exercise all three: mind, soul, and body.
Discover your inner lithe child
through the folds of your flesh;
recall the girl who ran madly through
the streets, because she wanted to
not because the police were chasing.
You are born with only one shell
tend it like a delicate butterfly garden
it is wild like the weeds but needs tending.

Anyway dear little sister, before
I come home to didaction do not do
the worst of what I've done and I hope
you learn and love and laugh as much as me
and cry because it comes as easily,
if you are soft at heart, and remember
to thine own self be true, because
this is where it's at, the truth.

September 3, 1999

In the Name of Maxwell Ali Trudell

Max, Max
get on back
to your body
punch like Ali
light on your feet
swift like a rooster,
beat the monster
strike with your will
and God's too,
(though you'll
probably be Agnostic).
Please baby please
live a little well,
a testament upon
our memories,
pad down the hallway
in your bare pajama feet
and land in our laps
with a leap from the stairs.
We crave to see your black curls
bounce to meet us
perched on top pop's shoulder
and watch you grow fat
off your mother's
semi sweet milk.
Please baby please
live on through the night,
fight with your Midwestern might,
remember your parents
and the people who loved you
long before you were born.
Please baby please
rage, rage against the
close of midnight.

November 12, 1999

In this Realm

No matter what I dream
I still breathe you
in the midnight hour
after a long winter's sleep,
I smell your male musk scent
touch your marble back
know before you exhale
and rollover to spoon
a little while before
work takes over
claims its toll
in exchange for
paltry dough.

December 1, 1999

We Asked Him To Stay But He Couldn't.....

Stage One

Pain pockets pulse inside
pierce me with bitter puss,
I cringe, cower at the normal world
I don't want no two-bit toothy grin
smile snapping back at me
while the unknown evil lurks too close,
for any instant action surgery, sedatives or sleep.

Stage Two

I'm telling this because she asked me:
my best friend's breasts hurt
laden with life's liquid
but there's no takers
most mornings she weeps
as she pumps away the excess
when she hugs her husband
they cry out, flood her shirt, grieving.

Stage Three

I feel my lover's pain
rack his body
shake it like a leaf
while he weeps,
so do I.
Devoted uncle
in life, in death
forever
Max Ali
on his chest.

Stage Four

My best friend,
her lover and mine,
we've all cried
until our eye sockets
have run dry,
tears fall like rain
in the desert,
evaporate but
leave traces.
This pain radiates

like electricity
tingles.
A profound
loss of faith
occurs, confounds
the race for the cure
from this illogical madness,
they are such good people
contemporary world saviors,
intensive care nurse,
social worker, socialists,
there is no magical serum,
there is no one who can
understand.....
I know this now,
Karma's out too,
and yet I breathe,
dream, sometimes
feel desire for what's
in front of me, love.

Stage Five

It's one month since
Max was delivered,
we love him
though he's missing
from our circle,
nine months he existed
before he was born, died
and became a figment
of our long existence.
Some days I wish we were
sitting by Mindy's hospital bed
waiting for a telephone call
from our men still
praying for a miracle
not stuck in this fifth dimension
this altered state of reality
where everything is fucked up
and will be for a long time.

December 16, 1999

Philosophy

I scare myself sometimes
but I know what's right and true;
like angels do exist
and there is a God,
a force in this universe
who wishes us well,
if there's a god at all, and
holy people do live, breathe,
walk the earth and leave,
and if there's good
then there's evil,
because to have one
you must have the other,
life in balance is rare;
also people do live forever
if only they'd remember
who they once were,
because hardly do we ever
make it to Nirvana,
though our souls
keep on trying
to climb to heaven's door
because evolution
commands it, demands it,
the reincarnation
of dirt, dust and matter
from seed to body
to breath to soil,
just like crawling
from water to land
to walk upright on
Earth's cradle crust
atmosphere;
but always this other
desire lurks near
hovering, whispering
sweet nothings in our ear
asking us please
come on home
we know Earth's
treasures are hard
to leave, but here
we'll give you shelter
from the storm.

1999

Chapter IV

New Beginnings

2000 to January 2001

The Secret Is

To remember to love the little things
like fresh 310 count
white cotton sheets,
warm spooning body heat,
the set of the red sun
on a mild summer day
when the flesh feels hot
from the rays of its
hopefully eternal,
internal combustion
and you can smell the man
laying next to you
feel his toasty skin
on the back of his neck
with your pin cushion lips
lick the salt off with your tongue
because you are connected
in a way that defies reality
you are flesh and blood soul-mates
swimming the stream life trying not
to get caught in the net of adulthood,
mortgages, diapers, and IRAs
until your whole life is on display
juggling like a puppet on a string,
for everyone to see, judge,
and you see life's like that
full of bullshit and all
but who cares it doesn't
have to stop there,
simple earth pleasures
like good food
can stoke your body
burn like it should
until the sweet aroma
of your own self consuming
wafts in to the room,
and you get high
off swallows of hearth
baked Italian bread
made this morning,
dipped in basil pesto spread
served with roasted garlic
and salmon frittatas,
and you don't care a fig
about your financial state
because you are basking

on a soft white beach
with your sweetie,
John Lee Hooker
sings the blues,
waves talk back to you,
your toes twist in the sand
keeping time while you melt,
baking dark brown,
true love child under the sun.

January 2000

Obituary for Tent City

(located six months at El Centro De La Raza on top of Beacon Hill)

Beacon Hill, the playground
the dirt, the lonely pavement
a stark area mourns the loss
of its recent inhabitants
the laughter, the tears,
the cries at night go unheeded
no one drives by
sees their plight across the lot
from Red Apple Grocery,
children, working people,
Latin, Black and White people
all lived here once
men and women
working together kept the peace
made a haven for the have-nots
voices, flashlights, sounds of love,
and soft dark light filtered
from inside their tents
survivors include cold-blooded
city permit enthusiasts.

January 22, 2000

Blessed Be Creation

I see a man around town sometimes
he can often be found
watching the sun set from a park bench,
he has spoke to me twice
I wrote this for him:
in the orange sherbet sky
pink and purple rays glide by
brick and mortar
soars towards the Sound,
this is what I love about being alive
the colors of the night.
I turn from my height
high above the city
in Jose Rizal Park
arch my neck
see the full moon rise
on the other side.
I sigh, exhale, glad to be living
in a free world
where I can see,
walk unencumbered,
where I don't pay to inhale
the honeysuckle breeze
floating off the lilac trees,
the roses, the sea
to land a smile on my face,
swelling heart, lips, brain,
with eve's scent of the season
the sweet smell of red, gold, and green
the coming black light.

April 24, 2000

At Play

When we were eleven and twelve seemed far away,
we met at a rival softball game,
opponents at play beginning our own,
I saw in your cerulean blue eyes a child
I had not met before, caliber undone,
someone who's just begun her intellectual journey,
a beacon brain on the eastside of Des Moines,
she did not yet know her own worth,
her own greatness in the marble urn of loss,
for hours we circled the field where we'd just played
and became conversant through conversation,
dirt caked, mud, mustard and candy encrusted
we begged our parents to let us spend the night together;
later armed with your sleeping bag and prayers
you came over and the curtain rose by seventh grade.

April 24, 2000

Making Sense

Like trees we cling by our roots to what's grounded
especially in a full gale wind – connections,
this is what we need to survive life's pitfalls,
to drink and survive far beneath the desert surface
of this artificial world, sink our teeth into some depth, our past,
understand who we once were, who we are today, how we got here,
these are the thoughts we need to ruminate upon first
to become larger than our minute selfish selves craving
attention at all times to become greater than our own basic needs.

April 24, 2000

Honor Before Waking

Swimming between the sheets
in the wee hours of the morning
I whimper in my sleep
when I see my dear mom drowning:
we walk on a narrow bridge ledge she slips
the water covers the black top of her head
her long trench coat swirls around
dragging her body down,
I tear off my coat
prepare to jump in save her
when my man wakes me
from my bad trip
murmurs still asleep,
"you're ok sweetie, it's just a nightmare,"
I rollover quick say a prayer,
thanks for the man who watches
over me while we are both dreaming.

April 25, 2000

That's Cool, Whatever

Let it ride baby,
let's not think 'bout tomorrow,
let's passion play, tell love stories,
mistakes other people make,
let us concentrate on ourselves,
our art, separately, you do your thing,
I'll do mine, then we can meet
for a tete-a-tete on the silk couch at night
for a glass of white wine, a smoke and a
tongue twine about life's true meaning.

May 16, 2000

November Pangs

Pain etched in the memory of my soul billows out
when the cold winds blow in November and I remember
when a black hole first became lodged in my heart,
in my throat, my whole being spent with disbelief,
our minds had held such thoughts, wishes withered,
our lips dried up where once your name sailed,
we couldn't accept defeat, medical science agreed,
and our hearts sunk to our feet as we waited the days
for you to take this vacant baby seat beside us,
grace us with your presence, your eyes, your smell,
for us your name is forever linked with the stars
and you are far, far away having slipped out
in the middle of the night without our consent, little one,
who didn't get to die an old death like your peers,
we hope to see you in the next realm, dear heart,
maybe you'll be the same age as you were when you left
and we the wilder ones who got to revolve around the planet
will get to make up for lost time as your kin and parents.

November 1, 2000

White Washer Plant Town

When he was young
and growing up in that
white washer plant town,
he was scared
because "they" said,
"Them nuclear bombs
out there can kill ya',
so y'all better beware
and buy this here bomb shelter,
plant it in your back yard,
if'n you got one,
to protect you and yours,
from the nuclear fear fallout
from the goddamn KGB commies
before they be knocking down
the USA Corporate door with their
anti-capitalist red scare tactics,
with one touch of the button
they'll blow your house down,
you know they will."
Well, those farmers, Maytag-ers,
but not the one-armed railroaders
bought them up in a flash,
his little brown boy thought was,
"Shit, what about us?
Who'll take care of us?
We'll die out here."

December 17, 2000

Identity

White-Mexican looks like a Latina,
not my label
a question
from a Guatemalan student
who's come undone
in my ESL class,
doesn't get my kind
I try to describe
how I grew up
in Caucasian corn country
surrounded by houses
on cul-de-sacs
that all looked the same,
how we were alone
in a town of 5000,
one black family,
one Indian family,
one Asian family,
and one household of Mexicans,
no two, us and the Renterias
to whom we were related by marriage
before and after my divorce,
and they were mixed;
still, it was a good living,
happy in our cocooness,
our oneness,
separated by money
one direction
color on the other:
classes, classes, classes,
day and night
we took lessons:
piano, jazz, tap, ballet,
the dance team, trumpet,
trombone, tennis, Finishing School,
and one awful summer golf;
Christened, Confirmed, Cathechismized;
it all cut me in several places,
molding of head and heart
making me ultrasensitive,
then and now,
an observer of the outside,
an outsider among my own kind,
my very shade,
mysterious aloof
black haired beauty

who can't speak Spanish,
living among blue eyed dyed blond bombshells,
who held up her head higher
because she's shy not stuck-up,
understood, undenied, sacrificed to at any price
by my beloved little brown parents
who taught me well
gave up so much
so their daughters could shine
and they'd swell with pride
at the life they had given us,
on Sundays we basked
in mutual admiration after mass
singing our church songs while making breakfast,
according to the unspoken doctrine in our house of:
fast first eat later after communion,
we intruded with our Mexican music
bellowing out the open windows
the smell of bacon frying,
pancakes baking, coffee
and eggs scrambled to order
it wafted out on beautiful summer mornings
out of our house in Pleasant Hill, Iowa,
perched on the highest spot
one could reach on the East Side of the street
for first and second generation immigrants.

January 25, 2001

About the Author:

Angie Trudell Vasquez began writing when she was seven years old. She is a third generation Mexican-American from Iowa on her mother's side and second generation on her father's side. Her family arrived in Iowa in the late 1800's with the railroads and her father was the first person in the family to go to college. She received her literary education by reading books way too advanced for her as a child and more formally at the University of Iowa, Des Moines Area Community College and Drake University. A Ruth Lilly Poetry Fellowship finalist in 1995 she has written two books of poetry, ***The Force Your Face Carries*** and ***Love in War Time***. In 2003 she was a featured poet at Bumbershoot, Seattle's annual music and arts festival. As a member of Los Nortenos in the Pacific Northwest she produced many literary art shows for the group including a Peace Show benefit in 2005. Her work has appeared on stage at the Miracle Theatre Main Stage in Portland, Oregon and in print in The Raven Chronicles, Real Change, Stand Alone and Nerve House to name a few. She performs annually with the ACLU of Wisconsin's The Other America Tour and has taught poetry classes at Milwaukee's Woodland Pattern Book Center to adults and children. She's a co-founder of Art Night Books with her cartoonist husband Devin Trudell.